Essential Phonetics
for English Language Teachers

Tony Penston

tp TP Publications

TP Publications
59 Applewood Heights
Greystones
Co. Wicklow
Ireland

www.tppublications.com

© Tony Penston 2015

First published 2015

ISBN: 978 0 9531323 3 1

All rights reserved. No part of this publication may be reproduced, stored in a retrieval system or transmitted in any form or by any means without the prior written permission of the copyright owner.

Cover design by Kevin Brooks
Cover background © Shutterstock
Diagrams by the author
Printed by Ross Print, Greystones, Ireland

Thanks

I am very grateful to the following for their reviews of the manuscript: Gina Ball of Kangnam University, Yongin, South Korea; Rafaela Bepe of The British College of Brazil, São Paulo; Stephen Black of PACE Language Institute, Bray, Ireland; Jonathan Clayden of Eurocentres London; Liet Hellwig of Vancouver Community College, Canada; Peter Lahiff of Future Learning Ireland, Dublin; Sandra Reid of ATC Language and Travel, Dublin; Maura Walsh of Rotterdam University of Applied Sciences; John Whipple of ELT Makers, Dublin.
Special thanks to Rod Mitchell of Cactus WorldWide, Brighton & Hove, UK, for his generous correspondence on many items.
Thanks also to Pauline Brooks and Patricia O'Neill for pre-printing assistance.

CONTENTS

Introduction		5
1	**Terminology**	**7**
1.1	Phonetics	7
1.2	Phonology	7
1.3	Phonemics	8
1.4	The IPA	8
2	**Consonants**	**9**
2.1	Externally visible	9
2.2	Position of the velum; nasal articulation	10
2.3	Voiceless and voiced	10
2.4	Consonant chart and examples	11
3	**Difficulties with consonants**	**13**
3.1	Voiceless plosives (/p/, /t/, /k/) – aspiration	13
3.1.1	Aspiration on the following letter	14
3.1.2	Position dictates aspiration	14
3.1.3	'p' and 'b' highlighted	14
3.2	The 'l' and 'r' difficulty	15
3.2.1	L1 phonological rules	15
3.2.2	Articulation – drawing is often best	15
3.2.3	Articulation of 'l'	16
3.2.4	Articulation of 'r'	16
3.2.5	Clear 'l' and dark 'l'	16
3.2.6	Minimal pairs – creating	17
3.2.7	Minimal pairs – drilling	17
3.3	The 's' and 'sh' difficulty	18
3.3.1	Articulation of /s/	18
3.3.2	Articulation of /ʃ/ 'sh'	18
3.4	The Spanish L1 'v' and 'b' difficulty	19
3.5	Intervocalic lenition in Spanish	19
3.6	Past tense forms	20
3.7	Cats, dogs and horses	20
4	**Connected Speech**	**21**
4.1	Same or similar consonants	21
4.2	Assimilation	21
4.3	Elision	21
4.4	Consonant 'hopping'	21
4.5	Vowel to vowel: linking [j]	22
4.6	Vowel to vowel: linking [w]	22
5	**Vowels**	**23**
5.1	Description	23
5.2	The front two of the four 'corner' vowels	23
5.2.1	Articulation of /iː/	23

5.2.2	Articulation of /æ/	23
5.3	The back two of the four 'corner' vowels	24
5.4	The four corner vowels on the vowel chart	24
5.5	All monophthongs on the vowel chart(s)	25
5.6	List of monophthongs	26
5.7	Notes on the vowel charts	27
5.7.1	The central vowel phonemes and low front vowel	27
5.7.2	The GA chart	27
5.8	Diphthongs	28
5.9	Hear phonemes and more online	28
6	**Difficulties with vowels**	**29**
6.1	/iː/ as in *sheep* and /ɪ/ as in *ship*	29
6.2	Repairing is tiring	30
6.3	/iː/ as in *seven<u>teen</u>* and /i/ as in *<u>seventy</u>*	30
6.4	/uː/ as in *fool* and /ʊ/ as in *full*	31
6.5	Other vowel difficulties	32
6.6	Diphthongs: lack of prominence on first element	33
6.7	Diphthongs: pronounced as monophthongs	33
6.8	Influence of final consonant on preceding vowel	33
6.9	Role play script: voiceless/voiced final consonant	35
6.10	The schwa: /ə/	36
7	**Suprasegmentals**	**37**
7.1	Stress/emphasis, rhythm	37
7.2	Contrastive stress	38
7.3	Pronouns, and the conjunction *that*	38
7.4	Marking the stressed syllables	39
7.5	Three degrees of stress	40
7.6	Stress in words	41
7.7	Phrasal verbs	41
7.8	Compounds	41
8	**Intonation**	**42**
8.1	Tone movements and meanings	42
8.2	The tonic syllable	42
8.3	Given and new information	43
8.4	Try storytelling	44
8.5	'Ham up' role play for intonation practice	44
9	**Accent**	**45**
9.1	Teachers have different accents	45
9.2	Native speaker accent	45
10	**Using phonemes in class**	**46**
10.1	To dispel ambiguity	46
	The International Phonetic Alphabet	47
	Bibliography	48

Introduction

A compact book
This booklet is written mainly for English language teachers who can pronounce anything in English perfectly but are unsure of their skills in and their approach to pronunciation teaching. It may also be suitable for inclusion on a TEFL/CELTA teacher training course. My intention is simply to help teachers build their skills in identifying the causes of spoken errors and facilitating their correction with confidence and efficiency. Thus, much of what would normally be contained in a phonetics course can be dispensed with or minimised. This even includes audio accompaniment, though we do include directions to online sources. Such trimming facilitates the creation of this extraordinarily compact book.

An essential component of continuous professional development
The envisaged reader is the holder of a Certificate in English Language Teaching (to adults) or is participating on such a course. Certificate courses typically have insufficient time to include a comprehensive treatment of phonetics; consequently, many in-service teachers, graduates of such courses, soon notice their lack of ability to analyze and explain the cause of an error and correct it through phonetically oriented techniques, the need for which would be evidenced by frustrated students. Teachers in such a situation will likely recommend a pronunciation book or online practice programme, but it's a fact that most students expect their teacher to be able to help them with *all* their learning difficulties. Face-to-face learning, imperfect as it may be, would seem to be preferred over the 'perfect' yet impersonal digital alternative.

Continuous professional development programmes should include as an essential component pronunciation teaching with phonetic awareness. The teacher armed with a knowledge of how sounds are articulated and which symbols represent those sounds has a much better chance of identifying learner errors and aiding in their correction than one with the 'listen and repeat' method only.

American, British
A welcome feature of this book is the consideration shown to speakers of GA (General American) along with the featured GB (General British) and other varieties of English. The inclusion of two vowel charts (GB and GA) is a first, as is the use of images in a vowel chart to indicate rounded vowels. The 'Global English' teacher is used to moving between GA and GB, the choice dictated by coursebook and/or environment. A native speaker accent is not the target in modern language teaching, but the modern language teacher must be phonemically au fait with the different mainstream accents in order to teach pronunciation confidently.

Extendable knowledge
Of course only a representative sample of common mispronunciations can be dealt with in this booklet. However, upon reading, the teacher will be able to apply the acquired knowledge and skill to the treatment of most other areas of difficulty.

Just in case...
In case the reader is under the misapprehension that the teaching of individual sounds is of low priority in ELT, we would point out that in a widely reported study the majority of breakdowns in communication between non-native speakers were caused by mispronunciation, not grammatical or lexical errors; and individual sounds, not suprasegmentals, were at the heart of these errors (Jenkins 2000: 88). In the classroom the evidence that pronunciation knowledge assists both the listening and writing skill is indisputable. And as for the reading skill we would draw the reader's attention to 'Phonology in second language reading: not an optional extra' (Walter 2008).

Shortcuts
In order to maintain brevity I have taken some licence with the English language. For example there may be some deliberate grammatical errors caused by conflating sentences, and lack of punctuation between phonemes and graphemes or example words. Also for the sake of brevity the explanation of some terms may not accompany their introduction; the context will often be of sufficient assistance but failing this the reader should look ahead to where the explanation will follow. The Contents section is deliberately detailed to aid in any search.

Abbreviations
AuE	Australian English pronunciation.
GA	General American English pronunciation.
GB	General British English pronunciation (see RP below).
IrE	Irish English pronunciation (sometimes known as Hiberno-English).
L1	First/native language, mother tongue.
L2	Second/foreign/target language.
RP	Received Pronunciation, a 'posh' British accent. The abbreviation is now being replaced by GB, representing an accent used by a wider range of speakers but still recognised as standard.
ScotE	Scottish English pronunciation (author's abbreviation – the standard is ScE).
Ss	Students.

1 Terminology

1.1 Phonetics

Phonetics is the study of all language sounds, how we produce and hear them. **Acoustic phonetics**, how language sounds are represented by sound waves, can be useful for technological and identification purposes, but **articulatory phonetics**, how we move the vocal articulators such as lips, tongue, vocal cords, etc, would be our main instrument when explaining language sounds in the classroom.

1.2 Phonology

Phonology concerns the rules (= generally accepted pronunciation norms) of a particular language, and its inventory of sounds. One rule of English is that it can have a **cluster** of three consonants as in, for example, *spleen, asks, risked*, but can't have initial 'n' or 'm' plus consonant, as in *mtoto*, the Swahili for *child*. Another rule, for many non-rhotic speakers (those who don't pronounce the 'r' in *card*, etc.) is the **linking intrusive 'r'** rule, which applies when one word ends in a certain vowel and the following word starts with a vowel, e.g. *Thelma-r-isn't here; no law-r-against it* (the word *law* ends in a vowel sound, despite what the consonant letter tells you). This may extend to *drawing* being pronounced as *draw-r-ing*, etc.

A Chinese phonological rule is that a word can start with an 'l' but not an 'r', and can end with an 'r' but not an 'l'. Korean words can end with an 'l' but not an 'r'. A Turkish rule is that certain vowels must harmonise with the previous vowel.

Korean has no /f/ phoneme, Arabic has no /b/ phoneme. Spanish has no /v/ phoneme, English has no /ø/ phoneme (as in the French *ceux*, 'those'). And as you may know, quite a lot of languages but especially the Romance (Latin based) ones have /i:/ as in *beet* but not /ɪ/ as in *bit*, hence the 'sheep or ship' difficulty. Etc.

Obviously, knowing your learner's L1 can be of benefit when teaching, but of equal or greater importance is your ability to hear errors, to ascertain the cause and to help your learner eradicate them. I believe a knowledge of articulatory phonetics to be essential for this.

1.3 Phonemics

In simple terms a phoneme is a minimal sound that can change the meaning of a word. For example /t/ and /d/ are phonemes in English because *cat* /kæt/ and *cad* /kæd/ have different meanings, but the alveolar tap/flap (like the quick Spanish 'r') for the /t/ in *better* in GA (General American English), represented by [ɾ] or [t̮], is not a phoneme because it doesn't change the meaning of the word. For some GB (General British English) speakers, mainly with the 'Estuary English' accent, the /t/ in *better* and *but* is realized as a glottal stop, a sudden stop in breathing, represented by [ʔ], and for most southern Irish English and some Australian (Melbourne) English speakers the same /t/ is realized as a type of retroflex* alveolar fricative (like 'r' and 's' together), which may be represented by [ṣ]. Finally, Liverpudlians, using their 'scouse' accent, pronounce a final /t/ as [ts].

Retroflex means a backward movement of the tongue tip. *Alveolar fricative* means there is some 'friction' or hissing sound made between the tongue and the alveolar ridge (the ridge behind your front teeth). See page 9 for places of articulation and page 11 for consonant types.

We all might swear we pronounce the phoneme /t/ as the standard alveolar plosive that the symbol represents, [t], but the fact is we don't all pronounce the same phoneme in the same way, especially when it occurs in different parts of a word. Note: phonemes are enclosed by slash marks / / and their realizations, the sounds we actually make, are represented by symbols enclosed by brackets [ ]. And the word for the realizations is *allophones*. As a final example, the dental [t̪] is an allophone used by many Irish English speakers for 'th', the phoneme /θ/. Relax, that's the end of this lesson on allophones. But in passing it should be added that, at least when teaching English as a lingua franca, there's little need to insist on the precise 'th' pronunciation (Walker, 2010, p29).

1.4 The IPA

The International Phonetic Alphabet is a chart of all speech sounds. Included would be the Spanish tapped or flapped 'r' /ɾ/, the Hausa ejective click /k'/, the Arabic voiced pharyngeal fricative /ʕ/, etc, but as we are mainly interested in English phonemes we'll dispense with other languages for now. A reproduction of the IPA is on page 47. Charts of English consonants and vowels appear later below.

2 Consonants

2.1 Externally visible

Only a few consonant articulations are visible, demonstrable. They include the tongue lightly touching the teeth for the 'th' sound, either the voiceless 'th' /θ/ in <u>th</u>ink, wid<u>th</u>, or the voiced 'th' /ð/ in <u>th</u>is, wea<u>th</u>er; also the lower lip meeting the upper teeth for the voiceless labiodental /f/ ('labia' = lips) or the voiced version /v/. Diagrams of these articulations but especially of articulations made further back in the vocal cavity and therefore not demonstrable may be found in the popular pronunciation books and on the Internet; some also in this book.

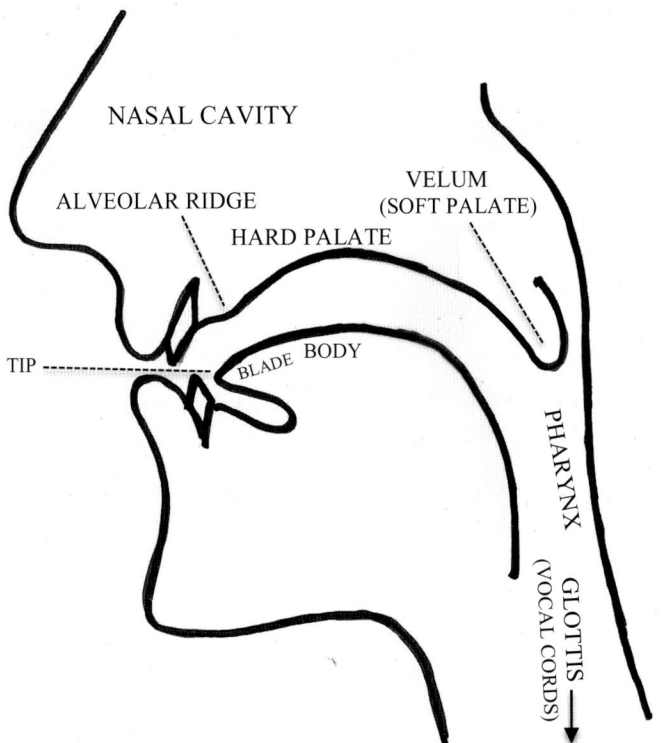

Figure 1: Main articulators in the vocal tract. Phoneticians use the term *front*, but I prefer 'body' for that part of the tongue behind the blade. Lips and teeth are not deemed to require labelling here.

2.2 Position of the velum; nasal articulation

In the above diagram you will see that the velum is lowered, allowing air to enter the nasal cavity. To notice the movement from non-nasal to nasal say *lightning* very slowly. For the 't', the velum is raised against the back wall of the pharynx, blocking air entry into the nasal cavity while the tongue, pressing against the alveolar ridge and side teeth, blocks air from escaping through the mouth. Then for the 'n' the velum is lowered, air enters the nasal cavity and the alveolar nasal consonant /n/ is pronounced.

Many GA speakers nasalize vowels before nasal consonants, like the /æ/ in *tan, cram* or *bang*, or the /e/ in *them*. Portuguese L1 learners may tend also to nasalize vowels in similar contexts, but to the extent of leaving the nasal consonant, if it is final, inaudible.

2.3 Voiceless and voiced

- *Voiceless* is when the vocal cords are open, allowing air to pass through without vibration, and the vocal tract muscles are tense.
- *Voiced* is when the vocal cords are vibrating and the vocal tract muscles are relaxed.

For most consonants *tense* and *lax** work better for me than *voiceless* and *voiced*. That's why I have underlined the relevant phrases above. Hear and feel the difference by saying the words below, slowing down on the underlined letters, while blocking your ears with your fingers:`

voiceless (tense)	voiced (lax)
'th' /θ/	'th' /ð/
think	*this*
width	*weather*
teeth	*teethe*
'f' 'ph' 'gh' /f/	'v' /v/
safe/graph/rough	*save*

Instead of *save*, above, *saver* would be a better example for 'voiced', because /v/ and other voiced consonants become devoiced in word final position. Try it as instructed above for comparison.

*The standard terms are *fortis* and *lenis*, but *tense* and *lax* (or for Ss, *relaxed*), normally used with vowels, would seem more 'user-friendly' with consonants also.

2.4 Consonant chart and examples

Take a look at the consonants in the chart below. Observe that the place of articulation goes from the left of the vocal tract (the lips) to the right (the glottis). Figure 2 on page 9 explains *glottis* and other articulators visually. Now look for /f, v/ (*p*_h_*ase*, *v*_ase_) and /θ, ð/ (*th*_ink_, *th*_is_). You will notice that these pairs of sounds are articulated in the same place in your mouth, but the first member of each pair is voiceless (tense) and the second is voiced (lax).

Now look at /p, b/ (*rap*_id_, *rab*_id_). These also have the same contrast, i.e. voiceless and voiced. However, there's little noticeable voicing with /b/, especially in word initial or word final position, so you may find it better to use the term 'relaxed' or 'lax' for it when comparing it with the voiceless, or 'tense', /p/ (see 3.1); similarly for /t, d/ and /k, g/. The other pairs also have the voiceless ~ voiced contrast, but the voiced members – v, ð, z, ʒ, and to an extent, d͡ʒ – can be pronounced with the vocal cords continually vibrating, so the description *voiced* sits well with them (see next page for example words with these phonemes). Ask students to tense and relax their vocal muscles accordingly to help with the pronunciation of voiceless and voiced consonants, if necessary.

The IPA chart for all vowels and consonants is on page 47.

The English consonants

	bilabial	labiodental	(inter)dental	alveolar	post-alveolar	palato-alveolar	palatal	velar	glottal
plosive/stop	p b			t d				k g	ʔ
nasal	m			n				ŋ	
fricative		f v	θ ð	s z		ʃ ʒ			h
affricate						t͡ʃ d͡ʒ			
approximant	w				r		j		
lateral				l					

Examples (excluding consonants already explained or not needing explanation) with occasional teaching tips:

/ʃ/   *shape, rash, ration, special, machine.*

/ʒ/   *measure, seizure, déjà vu, rouge.*

/t͡ʃ/   *watch, cheap, creature, cello.* For pronunciation difficulty first check that students can pronounce 'sh' /ʃ/ (see figure 6). Then ask them to pronounce the 't', slowly moving to the 'sh'. Write *t-sh* then *tshi:p* (*cheap*) on the board and drill a few times. After such narrow focus always move to useful sentences containing the phoneme for further practice, ensuring variety and 'added value'.

/d͡ʒ/   *badge, jeep.* For pronunciation difficulty first check that Ss can pronounce the /ʒ/ (see figure 7); there's no letter in English for this sound, so I use the phoneme itself. Then ask them to pronounce the 'd', slowly moving to the /ʒ/. Write *d-ʒ* then *dʒi:p* (*jeep*) on the board and drill. Move to more words then sentences for variety and value.

/j/   *yes, use.* Also in *pew* /pjuː/, *cute* /kjuːt/, *Tuesday* /tjuːzdeɪ/, etc. However, for /tj/ many speakers use /t͡ʃ/, e.g. /t͡ʃuːzdeɪ/ (which sounds like *chewsday*), etc. The GA pronunciation is /tuːzdeɪ/ – 'toozday', etc. (I'm not marking the stressed syllables at this stage.)

/ŋ/   *bring, brink.* We tend to think of this sound as always being represented by three letters, i-n-g, but you can see this is not so in *brink*, above, or *bank*, etc. We have fun when teaching *singer* and *finger* – you can go into morphophonemics if you like but "That's the way it is" works fine for me!

/w/   Some GA and many IrE and ScotE speakers also have /hw/, making a distinction between *Wales* and *whales*, for example.

[ʔ]   Glottal stop. A sudden closure of the glottis (vocal cords), used by some speakers, especially in SE England ('Estuary English') for the 't' in *but* or *bitter*, etc, also represented by the hyphen in *uh-oh*, also used (plosively) for emphasis with some vowel initial words, e.g. *ʔidiot!*, or generally to indicate surprise or shock. It features in German, careful speech, before initial vowels, also in Arabic, Korean and a number of other languages. It is not a phoneme in English.

3 Difficulties with consonants

Errors such as the Spanish L1 'gwould' instead of *would*, the Korean 'pine' instead of *fine*, the Brazilian Portuguese 'hacket' instead of *racket*, etc, will be assumed to be correctable by imitation and practice. Most of the errors dealt with in this book are ones that likely need more than just the 'listen and repeat' treatment.

3.1 Voiceless plosives (/p/, /t/, /k/) – aspiration

On the consonant chart (page 11) you will see 'plosive/stop' in the first row. This means that these consonants can start a word/syllable (plosive) or end it (stop). In fact they can have either name regardless of their position but it's good to distinguish them in this way for now. Apart from the glottal stop, which is not a phoneme in English, there are three voiceless plosives, /p/, /t/ and /k/.

English voiceless plosives in word-initial position are *aspirated*, i.e. said with a following burst of breath. Notice the difference between *pet* and *bet, tin* and *din, call* and *gall*. Many languages' voiceless plosives aren't aspirated and the difference between them and their voiced counterparts is made in other ways, but in English an initial voiceless plosive is always aspirated; if not, it is difficult to distinguish it from its voiced counterpart.

The typical way to demonstrate aspiration is to hold a piece of paper in front of your mouth and say *pay* and *bay*, etc. The paper should move on *pay* but not on *bay*. Have Ss try it. You could also put a superscript ^{h} after the *p, t* or *k* when you write on the board. Show (with the 'h') and pronounce an extended burst of breath after the consonant, slowly moving on to the vowel, then graduate to a normal pronunciation.

phh-ay   phh-ay p^hay t^heachers more.
He who p^hays the p^hiper c^halls the t^hune.

Figure 2: Boardwork showing aspiration indicators.

Another technique is to have students say 'hay', for example, a number of times, then pronounce 'p' (not 'pee', just a voiceless 'peh') followed by 'hay', then move the two together.

3.1.1 Aspiration on the following letter

Many learners will pronounce *played* almost as *blade*. Again, lack of aspiration is the cause of the error, and in this case the aspiration should carry onto the 'l'. Correct the error by showing the word with a superscript 'h' after the 'l' as in *pl^{h}ay* and pronounce an extended voiceless 'l' after the 'p'. Similarly with *cl^{h}ean*, etc, if required.

Other second letters to carry the aspiration are 'r' as in *pr^{h}ayed* (possibly heard, if pronounced without aspiration, as *braid* or *bread*), *tr^{h}y, cr^{h}aft,* and 'w' as in *kw^{h}ality* (*quality*). But as we maintain throughout, there's no need to base a lesson on 'suspected' difficulties. Wait to hear the error before correcting it!

3.1.2 Position dictates aspiration

We have said that voiceless plosives (/p/, /t/, /k/) are aspirated in word initial position, but in fact the aspiration occurs when they are in stressed syllable initial position:

Pl^{h}ease pr^{h}ay for the dep^{h}árted.

Because *-part-* is the stressed syllable in *departed* above, the 'p' is aspirated (I mark stressed syllables on the board with an accent).

Voiceless plosives have little or no apiration when in <u>unstressed</u> syllable initial position, e.g. the 't' in *depárted* above (or note the difference between the two 't's in *tótal*) or the 'p' in /ɪnˈsɪpɪd/ (dictionaries show primary stress with a preceding apostrophe). They are unaspirated following an 's', e.g. in *spell, mistake, discover*, etc.

3.1.3 'p' and 'b' highlighted

I have focused more on the 'p' and 'b' than the other pairs of plosives, because 1) more words begin with the letters in this pair, and 2) Arabic doesn't have two bilabial plosives ('p' and 'b'), just the one, close to the English 'p' but never aspirated; and some other languages don't have the same distinction between their labial plosives as English does.

I have seen the written work of Arabic L1 students contain errors like *We rowed the poat*, proving that the teaching of correct phonemic pronunciation would also help the listening skill and ultimately the writing skill, a point often overlooked in discussions on pronunciation teaching.

3.2 The 'l' and 'r' difficulty

3.2.1 L1 phonological rules
Phonological rules concerning the distribution of [l] and [r] in three Oriental languages are (roughly stated):
   Chinese can start a word with an 'l' but not an 'r', and can end a word with an 'r' but not an 'l'. (There is an initial 'r' but it's not the same as the English 'r', being a fricative /ʐ/.)
   Korean has a similar constraint but mainly in reverse, i.e. a word can end with an 'l' but not an 'r'; a small number of words start with 'r', none with 'l'. (To be precise, both the 'l' and 'r' sounds are represented by the same letter, which is pronounced either way according to the environment; this includes like a flapped 'r' between vowels and like an 'l' before a consonant.)
   Japanese has an 'in-between' sound for both, but more like an 'l' initially and an 'r' between vowels. It doesn't occur finally.

3.2.2 Articulation – drawing is often best
When a student pronounces 'l' instead of 'r' they are holding the blade of their tongue in contact with the alveolar ridge instead of just raising it towards but not touching the post-alveolar area (pronounce 'l' and 'r' yourself and feel the movement of the tongue). See figure 1 on page 9 and figures 3 and 4 on the following page for elucidation on these terms and articulations. Also read 3.2.3 and 3.2.4.

Use visuals to help students become aware of problem articulations. You can point to these while doing intensive practice routines such as minimal pairs (see 3.2.6-7). Using board drawings is much faster and less hassle than making photocopies or fussing with projector and equipment. It also engages students – you can elicit as you draw.

So, to work:
Just start drawing from the nose and follow to the end of the hard palate; there's usually no need to continue on to the velum (soft palate) or draw the back wall of the pharynx. Then start the lower part from the lower teeth, moving to the left and finishing with the chin. Finally, draw the tongue in its correct position for the phoneme, ideally using a different colour marker or chalk. After a few tries you will be able to do this in seconds, earning major respect from your students.

3.2.3 Articulation of /l/

The blade of the tongue makes contact with the alveolar ridge (the ridge behind the upper teeth). The sides of the tongue are brought in (indicated by the dotted line) to let the air escape laterally. Try pronouncing 'atl' of *at least* slowly to perceive this – the 't' stops air front and sides, then there is a 'lateral release' of the air.

3.2.4 Articulation of /r/

The tip of the tongue is raised to the post-alveolar region, but doesn't touch it. With some speakers it may be brought further back in a retroflex action. The back rims of the tongue are in contact with the upper molars, otherwise there is no impedence of air. The central part of the tongue is 'hollowed'.

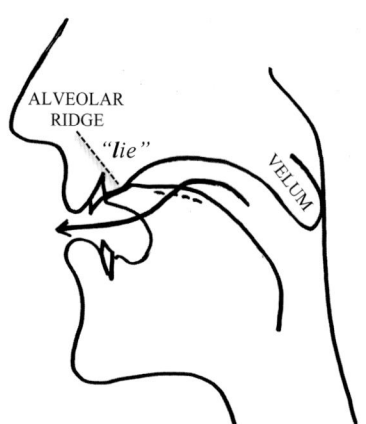

Figure 3: Articulation of /l/.

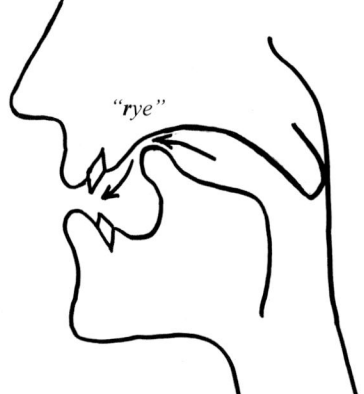

Figure 4: Articulation of /r/.

3.2.5 Clear 'l' and dark 'l'

In GB the 'l' tends to be 'clear', with the back of the tongue low, as in *live, filly* (before a vowel), or 'dark', with the back of the tongue high, as in *bill, film* (word final or before a consonant). However, GA, ScotE and AuE speakers generally prefer the dark 'l' for all positions, while IrE and West Indian English speakers prefer the clear 'l' likewise.

3.2.6 Minimal pairs – creating

Sets of minimal pairs can be found in popular student pronunciation materials such as *Ship or Sheep?* (Baker 2006); however, the pairs below will give you an idea of how to create your own. Just one phoneme makes the difference; try to vary its position in the word, and add more of the type that your Ss are struggling with.

Minimal pairs of 'l' and 'r'

towel	*tower*
pale	*pair**
palate	*parrot*
pilot	*pirate*
lice	*rice*
glamour	*grammar*
play	*pray*
bleed	*breed*
candle	*candour*
fanlight	*fan right***

*This is only a 'near minimal pair' as there is a difference in diphthongs, but the difference is hardly noticeable in some rhotic accents. It is included for its value as a word final example. Use more, like *pole - pour*, if the need is noted and the learned accent is rhotic.

**This is an example of a 'near minimal pair', included here to exemplify testing further configurations (in Japanese, 'n' may be followed by 'l' but not 'r').

3.2.7 Minimal pairs – drilling

Drill minimal pairs column by column and then row by row. Then have a discriminating task where you or a student calls out a word and another student (at the board) identifies it. Finally, introduce some sentences with the relevant phonemes: proverbs, idioms, quotations or extracts. Drill and have them learnt by heart. e.g.

All roads lead to Rome.
He who laughs last laughs longest.
I'm a real dyed-in-the-wool romantic.
All that glitters is not gold. (Shakespeare)
If it doesn't kill you it'll make you stronger. (Nietzche) (simplified)

I am Hamlet the Dane,
skull-handler, parablist,
smeller of rot. (Heaney)

3.3 The 's' and 'sh' difficulty

Some languages or dialects do not have the /s/ and /ʃ/ contrast as English does in *save* and *shave*. Some also do not have the /ʒ/ phoneme (as in *measure*). Use visuals of the vocal cavity, and practise with words and phrases to resolve any difficulties.

3.3.1 Articulation of /s/

The blade (not the tip) of the tongue is held very close to the alveolar ridge, almost touching it. Air escapes along a groove in the centre of the tongue and causes friction between the blade of the tongue and the alveolar ridge. The sides of the tongue are pressed against the upper side teeth.

/s/ (as in *peace, loose*) is voiceless; /z/ (as in *peas, lose*) is voiced, both having the same place of articulation.

3.3.2 Articulation of /ʃ/ 'sh'

The frontal body of the tongue is raised towards the palate. The sides of the tongue are in contact with the upper side teeth. The friction occurs over a larger area (mainly palatal) than that with /s/.

/ʃ/ (as in *mesh, cash*) is voiceless; /ʒ/ (as in *measure, casual*) is voiced, both having the same place of articulation.

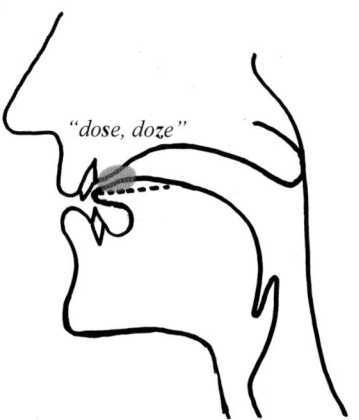

Figure 5: Articulation of /s/ or /z/.

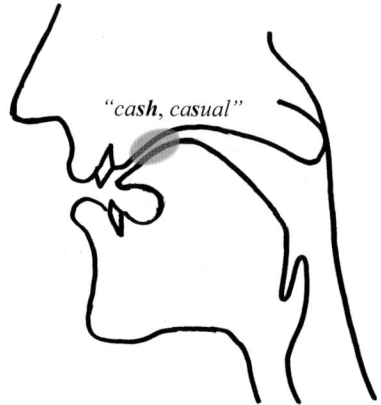

Figure 6: Articulation of /ʃ/ or /ʒ/.

3.4 The Spanish L1 'v' and 'b' difficulty

The Spanish phoneme /b/ is realized as [β] between vowels, and [b] when starting an utterance. But never as a [v]. The [β] may be heard as a voiced [v] by the teacher, but in fact it is not a labiodental articulation (which in the case of [v] would be lower lip to upper teeth) but simply a bilabial, an approximation of the lips. In Spanish, *robado* 'robbed' tends to sound like *rovado* or *rowado*. Hence *label* will sound a little like *layvel* or *laywell*, and *rob a boat* may be heard as *row a boat*. Practising the bilabial /b/ and labiodental /v/ in words and phrases of high frequency will help, but it may also be helpful for the learner to 'see' when a 'b' and a 'v' would be pronounced, as this is the nub of the issue. The strategy of visualising the word (when not reading it) before pronouncing it could pay dividends.

As we have said, the Spanish /b/ is realized as [b] in utterance initial position, so *Book the tickets* will be pronounced correctly. However, as there is no /v/ phoneme in Spanish, *Vary your repertoire* may be produced as *Bary your repertoire*, perhaps heard as *Bury your repertoire*, and *Vending machines will reduce costs* may be pronounced as *Bending machines will reduce costs*. To correct this error, besides practising the labiodental articulation, the learner may find it helpful to conjure up an image of the upper teeth as a 'V' meeting the lower lip, and to 'see' the word before pronouncing it.

Figure 7: Visual mnemonic. The 'v' (upper teeth) meets the lower lip.

3.5 Intervocalic lenition in Spanish

Just as the /b/ in Spanish is pronounced as a fricative (continuous, with some 'friction') between vowels (see *label* > *layvel* or *laywell* above), so also are the /d/ and /g/. Hence, *an adder* may be pronounced as [anaðə(r)], possibly mistaken for *another*, and *bigger* as [bɪɣə(r)], which may sound like *beer* said in a breathy voice. This frication may also occur at the end of words, e.g. *She had to begh*. Listen out for this and correct as appropriate.

3.6 Past tense forms

Past tense pronunciations are easily shown on the board. As you know, words ending in 't' or 'd' have a pronounced /-ɪd/ ending in the past tense form, which you may show as *want-wantid*, *land-landid*, etc. Then the other words require special treatment. I put a large 'T' after voiceless consonants and 'D' after voiced ones, e.g.

final voiceless consonant	final voiced consonant
skip – skipT	*rob – robbD*
miss – missT	*cause – cauzD*
risk – riskT	*beg – beggD*
fetch – fetchT	*cage – cage₍e₎D**
crash – crashT	–

*Sometimes it's necessary to retain the 'e' to avoid presenting the word with a new pronunciation, like 'cagd'.

The table above is for presentation here only; this technique is assumed to be used for correcting errors as they arise. If, however, a pronunciation lesson in past tense endings is earnestly requested by your students then you should oblige, but it would be vital to include meaningful sentences *(I ~~missed~~ missT you during the holidays)*, showing the normally spelled version of the focus word minimized and/or crossed out, situated ideally above the adjusted version. When drilling, gesture with clenched fists for the voiceless 'T' and with a calming gesture (palms downward) for the voiced 'D'.

When correcting a past tense form error stay with the consonant concerned, voiceless and voiced version if you like, but no other; the student may not like being ushered into an unrequested 'lesson' covering other consonants.

3.7 Cats, dogs and horses

Another example of 'voiceless/voiced' assimilation (see 4.2) is with the appended 's'. Observe: *cats, laps, bucks*, but *dogz, labz, bugz*. And then for ease of pronunciation, *horsiz* (and *washiz, switchiz, foxiz*), which mirrors *wantid*, above. There's no need to go into further detail here – what you need to do is listen out for errors and show and practise the correct form.

4 Connected speech

4.1 Same or similar consonants
Gas station is often pronounced, especially by Spanish L1 students, as *gas-estation*. Write and drill as **gass_tation** then **gasstation**. Likewise, to cure the habit of stopping between words like *won't tell*, show and drill **won?tell** – the (brief) glottal stop generally interests students. Again, unify and stretch the appropriate joining sounds in *serve five*, *lip balm*, etc, and show the glottal stop in *won't do*, *can't tell*, etc.

4.2 Assimilation
A sound can take on an aspect of an adjacent sound. For example, at normal speaking speed, *ten people* will be pronounced as *tempeople*, the 'n' preparing for the bilabial aspect of the 'p'. *Ban kissing* can be heard as *bang kissing*. Internally, *batman* becomes *bapman*, etc. Also, the voiced /v/ in *have to* becomes voiceless /f/, so when you hear a delay between *have* and *to* drill **haffta** or suchlike.

4.3 Elision
Some sounds become elided, lost, for example the 'd' in *wind down* (*wine down?*), *held tight* (*hell tight?*), *robbed jewellery* (*rob jewellery?*). Intensive listening exercises (dictation, dictogloss) often reveal difficulties with elision and other aspects of connected speech; carefully monitor, correct and drill. Beyond such 'hot' corrections there is little need for formal pronunciation lessons in this area.

4.4 Consonant 'hopping'
When one word ends in a consonant and the following word starts with a vowel, like *an apple*, *switched on*, *big old*, the consonant will be attracted to the vowel, i.e. the sound of the aforementioned is *a-napple*, *switch-don*, *bi(g)-gold* There is a tendency among certain learners to insert a glottal stop, even an 'h' between the words ("an happle"). The glottal stop may mistakenly lend emphasis to the following word, or just sound awkward, whereas the 'h' may cause the creation of an unintended word. This can be corrected with practice accompanied by visual assistance like that in the boardwork shown below. Drill *napple* then *anapple*, drill *don* then *switchdon* and similar.

A nápple ə dáy keeps thə dóctə rəwáy.

Figure 8: Two examples of *catenation*, what I call 'consonant hopping'. The second example may be known as *linking 'r'*. Note smaller size of the schwa. Stress marking and (rising-) falling final intonation line are included.

Be careful not to over-apply these strategies. For example *not old* may appear to be a candidate for similar treatment, but rewritten as *not-told* it would contain a phonological misrepresentation, because the plosive /t/ (and the other voiceless plosives /p/ and /k/) are normally fully aspirated (see 3.1) when in word initial position, e.g. in *told*, which is not the case here. If correction is required (of "stop-e-over", "not-e-ʔold", "break-hup", etc,) ensure that the linkage is made with an unaspirated /p/t/k/ or in the case of /t/ an alveolar tap [t] (see 1.3).

4.5 Vowel to vowel: linking [j]
When one word ends in a high front vowel ('ee' sound) and the following word starts with a vowel, there is a short linking [j] (this consonant glide is the 'y' in *you* or the first sound in *useful* or the letter 'u' – see pages 11 and 12). Hence *tee off* should be shown and drilled as *tee-yoff*, *many ancient buildings* as *many-yancient buildings*, etc. (see figure 9 below). This should rectify the error of inserting a glottal stop or 'h' between the words.

4.6 Vowel to vowel: linking [w]
When one word ends in a rounded vowel ('o' or 'u' type) and the following word starts with a vowel, there is a short linking [w]. Hence *are you in tonight*, *blue ice cream*, *who are you* and similar should be shown and drilled as *Are youwin tonight*, *bluewice cream*, *whoware you*. This should rectify the error of inserting a glottal stop or 'h' between the words.

Don't cry ʸover spilt milk.

blue ʷice cream

Figure 9: Boardwork for vowel-to-vowel linking.

There are many other difficulties with consonants. We don't have enough space to deal with them, but we hope that having read the above you will be better able to identify errors and help your students correct them.

5 Vowels

5.1 Description

Vowel sounds are described according to the position of the highest point of the tongue (not the tip or blade, mind, but the body of the tongue itself) and the shape of the lips.

5.2 The front two of the four 'corner' vowels

Take a look at the position of the tongue for /iː/ as in *beet* and /æ/ as in *bat*.

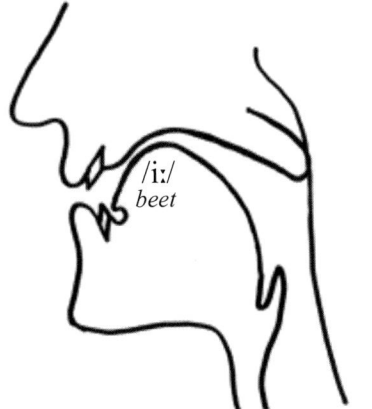 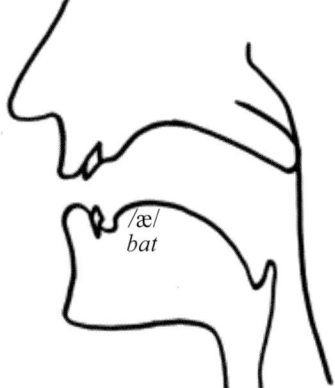

Figure 10: Articulation of /iː/.   Figure 11: Articulation of /æ/.

5.2.1 Articulation of /iː/

The highest point of the tongue is close to the palate (note: the tip of the tongue is low, close to or touching the back of the lower teeth). As the tongue is high in the mouth and near the front this is called a high front vowel.

5.2.2 Articulation of /æ/

Now if you make the sound /æ/ as in *sat*, you will have moved the highest point of your tongue close to the bottom of your mouth, but still towards the front. This is called a low front vowel. You will notice that the jaw drops with the tongue.

Essential Phonetics   23

5.3 The back two of the four 'corner' vowels

The other two corners of the mouth for vowels are the low back vowel, /ɑː/ as in *card* (also as in *call* for some non-GB accents) and the high back vowel /uː/ as in *cool*. Say these vowels slowly and become aware of the movement of your tongue and lips – the lips are rounded for /uː/ as indicated in the diagram.

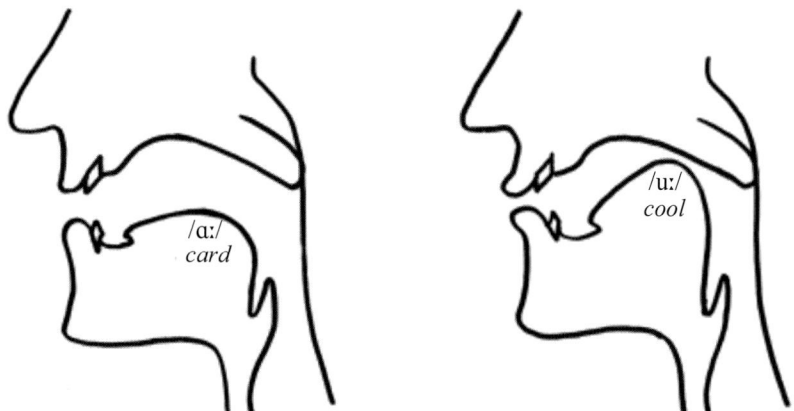

Figure 12: Articulation of /ɑː/.   Figure 13: Articulation of /uː/.

5.4 The four corner vowels on the vowel chart

We shall now see how these four vowels are represented on a vowel chart. The vowel chart roughly corresponds to scans taken of the mouth (facing left), marking the highest point of the tongue for each English vowel. The /æ/ is not quite at the bottom – there is a lower vowel [a] used by many speakers.

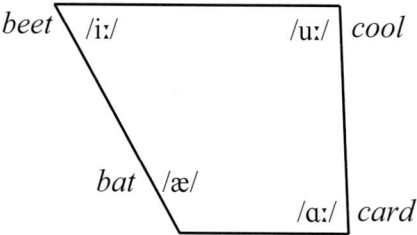

Figure 14: The four 'corner' vowels.

5.5 All monophthongs on the vowel chart(s)

All the English monophthongs (pure/single vowels – not diphthongs) are represented on the vowel charts below. Lip rounded vowels have adjacent visuals (only the second member of /əʊ/ is rounded).

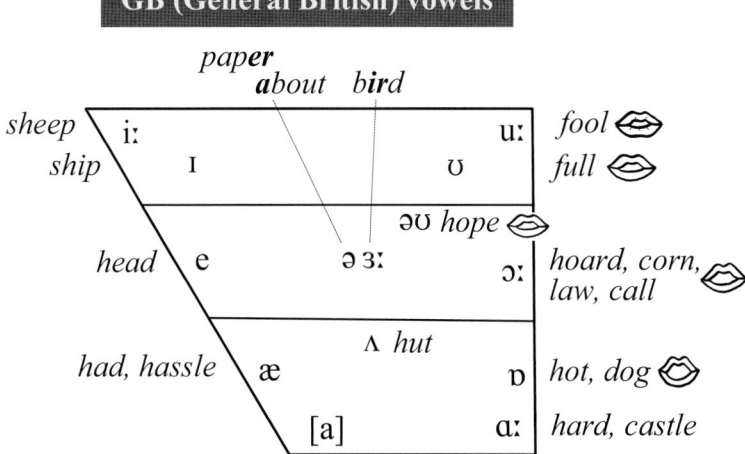

Figure 15: Vowel chart of GB monophthongs. One diphthong, /əʊ/ as in *hope*, is included for comparison purposes (see 5.8).

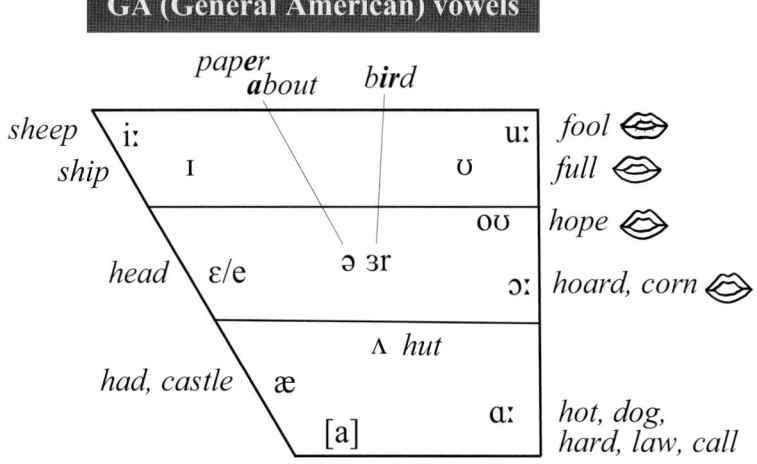

Figure 16: Vowel chart of GA monophthongs. One diphthong, /oʊ/ as in *hope*, is included for comparison purposes (see 5.8).

Essential Phonetics 25

5.6 List of monophthongs

Here's a list of the GB English monophthong vowels with example words and notes on other accents.

/iː/   *beet, beat, marine, obscene.* The short version /i/ is used for *happy, ready, chariot.*

/ɪ/   *bit, women, repeat, December, become.*

/e/   *bet, any, ready, said.* The symbol /ɛ/ is preferred by many American dictionaries; it represents a lower vowel than /e/ but the difference is hardly noticeable.

/æ/   *sat, patch, hassle.* The symbol /a/ is used by some American phonologists, though it represents a lower vowel.

/e/   *bet, any, ready, said.* The symbol /ɛ/ is preferred by many American dictionaries.

/æ/   *sat, patch, hassle.* The symbol /a/ is used by some American phonologists, though it represents a lower front-central vowel.

/ɑː/   *castle, pass, laugh, advance, card, father.* In GA, AuE, ScotE and IrE the vowel /æ/ is often used, but less so for *card, father.*

/ɒ/   *pot, stop, what.* In GA and IrE the vowel /ɑ/ is regularly used.

/ɔː/   *pour; saw, law, call, sought, taught.* In GA and IrE *saw, law, call, sought, taught* are often pronounced with /ɑː/.

/ʊ/   *put, bull, good, book.*

/uː/   *rule, food, soup.*

/ʌ/   *putt, bus, much, buck, front, flood.* In most southern Irish and northern English accents the vowel is closer to /ʊ/, making homophones or near homophones of *put* ≈ *putt, book* ≈ *buck, look* ≈ *luck.* There is occasional hypercorrection when *book* /bʊk/ is pronounced as /bʌk/ *buck.*

/ɜː/   *bird, her, work, nurse, fir, fur, fern.* In ScotE *bird* and *fir* are both pronounced with /ɪ/, while *fur*, and *fern* are pronounced with /ʊ/ and /e/. In southern IrE *fir, fur, fern* are also pronounced with /ɪ/, /ʊ/ and /e/, but *bird, her, work, nurse* are all pronounced with /ʊ/.

/ə/   *letter, doctor, cellar, about, o'clock, comfortable, desperate, camera, disposable, responsible, cactus.* (See 6.10)

5.7 Notes on the vowel charts

5.7.1 The central vowel phonemes and the low front vowel

The central vowels /ə/ and /ɜː/ actually represent the same sound (apart from length in this case), but different symbols are used as these vowels operate so differently.

[a] is a very low front vowel, and I have included it on the charts because 1) teachers who write phonemes on the board in a pronunciation lesson should generally favour it instead of the /æ/, 2) it is preferred by a small number of phonologists, 3) it is pronounced instead of /æ/ by IrE and some other speakers, 4) it is also used by some AuE speakers in words like *card*.

5.7.2 The GA chart

While the GB chart is generally accepted as representing a 'standard' for British English pronunciation there is no similar agreement for an American English vowel system. My GA chart is what I hope represents the most useful selection from American English dictionaries, the most useful for teaching that is, of course.

Both *call* and *law* are transcribed with the rounded vowel /ɔː/ by over half of the online American dictionaries which I consulted. However, most of the audios of these words for the same dictionaries and on other American pronunciation websites sound the vowel much closer to the unrounded /ɑː/ so I have placed the words accordingly. Obviously, I'm ignoring the fact that, as in the GB inventory, there are 'prestige dialect' reasons for designating phonemes, and to this end the rounded option would be more appropriate for GA also, but this time I'm going with the people. My only rationale would be that English is being used more informally and 'prestige' may not be as strong a consideration for designation as it used to be. And I do know that *dog* is pronounced with a rounded vowel by many GA speakers, but I'm restricting it to the unrounded spot, simply to maintain the pattern.

American publications may not include the length marking (the colon) after /iː/, /uː/, etc. Some show the /iː/ and /uː/ as glides, using the symbols /iy/ and /uw/ (some diphthongs may also be shown as glides). I believe length marking is best retained in the classroom for its simplicity and broader application.

For the vowel in *bird,* etc, you may see /ɔ:r/ or /ər/ or even /ɚ/ used instead of /ɜr/. The symbol /ɚ/ represents the simultaneous pronunciation of schwa + 'r', which is known as an 'r-coloured vowel'.

5.8 Diphthongs
Diphthongs are pronounced by moving from one monophthong position to another. They form the vocalic element of one syllable.

Most accents		GB		GA
/eɪ/	male, mail, bay, great, veil	/əʊ/	no, sew, soap, soul	/oʊ/
/aɪ/	I, eye, fine, sign, sigh, buy	/ɪə/	dear, deer, pier	/ir/
/ɔɪ/	boy, oil	/eə/	pair, pear, where	/er/
/aʊ/	house, how	/ʊə/	tour, ensure, boor	/ʊr/

Here are five diphthongs as they might appear on a vowel chart:

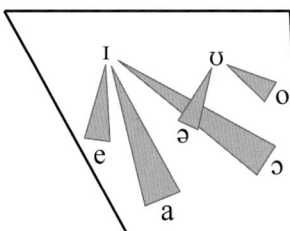

Figure 17: Diphthongs as in *bay* /beɪ/, *buy* /baɪ/, *boy* /bɔɪ/ and *beau* /bəʊ/ or in GA /boʊ/. Start and end positions of diphthongs may be a little different from their monophthong values.

There are just a few widely-heard diphthong variants:
AuE /eɪ/ is pronounced as /aɪ/ (*race* sounds like *'rice'*) and /aɪ/ is pronounced (roughly) as /ɑə/ (*rice* sounds like *'raw-ess'*); Canadian and IrE /aʊ/ is pronounced in certain positions as /ʌʊ/ or /əʊ/ (*house* /haʊs/ sounds like *'heh-ouse'*).

5.9 Hear phonemes and more online
If you wish to hear phonemes as you see them on a chart you can go online, either to one of the major ELT publishers (search with their name and 'pronunciation chart') or Youtube (search 'phonetic chart' etc.). To compare British and American pronunciations you can use online dictionaries. There are also apps which can record and assess your pronunciation.

6 Difficulties with vowels

6.1 /iː/ as in *sheep* and /ɪ/ as in *ship*

Again take a look at the position of the tongue for the vowel /iː/ as in *sheep, machine*, and now also for /ɪ/ as in *ship, result*.

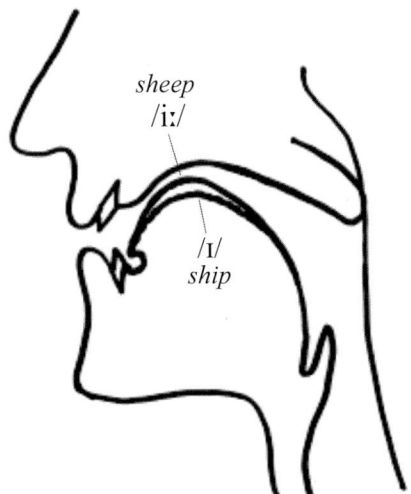

Figure 18: Articulation of /iː/ and /ɪ/.

For the pronunciation of /iː/ as in *sheep*:
1. The tongue (body, not tip) is high and towards the front – so close to the palate that there may be some friction.
2. The tongue is tense.
3. The sound is long (indicated by the colon after the 'i').
4. The lips are spread.

For the pronunciation of /ɪ/ as in *ship*:
1. The tongue is a little lower than for /iː/ and towards the centre.
2. The tongue is relaxed (I draw the tongue with a wavy line to suggest this – see figure 18). The technical term is *lax*.
3. The sound is short.
4. The lips are loosely spread.

As you can see in figure 18, the tongue positions for /iː/ and /ɪ/ are very close. In many other languages there is only one vowel in this area, roughly /i/. This allows for 'leeway'; for example in Spanish the word for 'wine' can be pronounced 'veeno' /viːnoʊ/ or 'vinno' /vɪnoʊ/ without fear of misinterpretation. This explains to a large extent the difficulty some students have in hearing and pronouncing the difference between the two vowels. For correction and practice it is necessary not only to show the image of the vocal cavity but also to inform of all the articulatory factors listed above.

Practising some '*sheep* and *ship*' words while concentrating on the above aspects should provide a good grounding for further work, normally comprising drilling minimal pairs (*sheep/ship, leave/live, leak/lick, bean/bin*), listening and discriminating between pairs and phrases, reciting short poems, doing short role plays, etc.

6.2 Repairing is tiring

Remember that breakdowns in communication are caused by more than exact minimal pair errors. Near minimal pairs like *see stairs* vs *sisters* should also be kept in mind. *Seem ball* could be heard instead of the intended *symbol, see stems* instead of *systems*, etc. Context will help correct the initial interpretation, but such repairing by the listener can become tiring, causing them to terminate the conversation early.

6.3 /iː/ as in *seventeen* and /i/ as in *seventy*

Another near minimal pair concerns the length of the vowel, in this case /i/. This vowel has full length in *key* /kiː/, *cheese* /tʃiːz/, etc, but is short at the end of *happy* /hæpi/, *twenty* /twenti/, etc. Now observe:
  seventéén /sevntiːn/ : *séventy* /sevnti/,
  sixtéén /sɪkstiːn/ : *síxty* /sɪksti/, etc.
Admittedly there is an 'n' to help with the distinction, but this is often pronounced so lightly as to be inaudible. To prevent mishearings the difference in vowel length (of /i/) should be emphasised. Awareness of the stressed syllable (see 7.5) of course is also important (I use an accent mark, as shown, to mark the primary stress on the board). Note that when the word is a numerical adjective the primary stress moves to the first syllable, e.g. *síxteen tons*, thus making the emphasis on vowel length even more imperative.

Many speakers make little difference in vowel length between such numerals. The result is constant requests for clarity by the listener. We can prevent our students from joining the offenders by building awareness and advocating a slight but expedient exaggeration.

6.4 /uː/ as in *fool* and /ʊ/ as in *full*

Take a look at the position of the tongue for these two vowels.

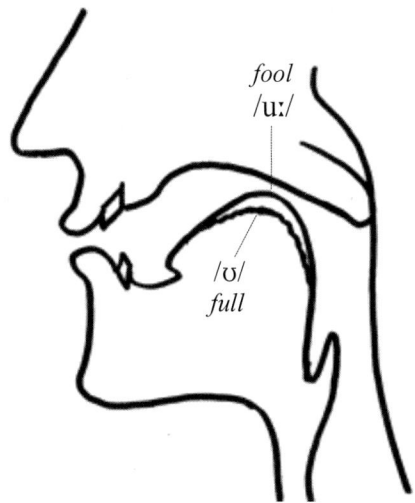

Figure 19: Articulation of /uː/ and /ʊ/.

For the pronunciation of /uː/ as in *fool*:
1. The tongue (body) is high and towards the back.
2. The tongue is a little tense.
3. The sound is long (indicated by the colon).
4. The lips are closely rounded.

For the pronunciation of /ʊ/ as in *full*:
1. The tongue (body) is a little lower than for /uː/ and a little towards the centre.
2. The tongue is relaxed (I draw the tongue with a wavy line to suggest this). The technical term for this type of vowel is *lax*.
3. The sound is short.
4. The lips are less rounded than for /uː/.

Like /iː/ *sheep* and /ɪ/ *ship* the tongue positions for /uː/ and /ʊ/ are very close, covering an area where many languages have just one vowel, /u/, and this would explain the difficulty some students have in hearing and pronouncing the difference between *pool* /uː/ and *pull* /ʊ/, etc. For correction and practice it is necessary not only to show the image of the vocal cavity but also to inform of the articulatory factors listed above. Regarding tenseness, although /uː/ is tenser than /ʊ/ it is not as tense as the symmetrical /iː/. The /uː/ of the students' L1 could have other differences from the English /uː/, such as degree and tenseness of lip rounding, tongue position and shape, but these are finer points.

Practising some '*fool* and *full*' words while concentrating on the above aspects, especially the difference in vowel length, should provide a good grounding for further work, normally comprising the drilling of minimal pairs (*pool/pull*, *suit/soot*, *Luke/look*), reciting short poems, doing short role plays, etc.

However, due to the much lower frequencies of /uː/ and /ʊ/ in text compared to /iː/ and /ɪ/ (/uː/ and /ʊ/ 1.99%; /iː/ and /ɪ/ 9.98% (Fry 1947)) you will find yourself attending to difficulties with the front rather than the back pair.

6.5 Other vowel difficulties

There are vowels in close proximity in the lower area of the vowel charts (see page 25) which often cause difficulty, e.g. GB /ɒ/ as in *shot* and /ʌ/ as in *shut*. Speakers with different accents have their own way of distinguishing between these, for example a GB speaker might emphasise the lip rounding of /ɒ/, whereas GA speakers who pronounce *shot* as /ʃɑːt/ (without lip rounding) may raise the tongue position for /ʌ/ (as in *shut*) towards the centre, moving it away from the /ɑː/, so to speak. The GB /æ/, as the ligature suggests, sounds half way between /a/ and /e/, keeping it a safe audible distance from /ʌ/, which can sound like an /a/, and so on. Use whatever technique works for you. But do show the position of the problem vowels on the vowel chart while practising; if you believe in the importance of visual, kinesthetic and auditive modes of learning then the benefits of this approach should be self evident.

6.6 Diphthongs: lack of prominence on first element

Most English diphthongs are pronounced with more prominence on the first element than the second. So, *fate* /feɪt/ is pronounced something like FAYt, not fayEET. Chinese doesn't have this distinction, consequently learners will first pronounce *fate* somewhat like *feet*, etc. Listen out, show the phoneme in the diphthong, in this case something like **féɪt**, and practice it with exaggerated prominence on the first element. Russian L1 learners also tend to put more or equal prominence on the second element rather than the first.

6.7 Diphthongs: pronounced as monophthongs

French L1 students often pronounce words like *fade* as *fed*. Similar reductions of diphthongs to monophthongs can be heard from other L1 students, including Italian, German, Thai. Showing the phonemes with some basic practice, and monitoring over time, will resolve the issue.

6.8 Influence of final consonant on preceding vowel

Pronounce the words in italics below (left to right):

voiceless final consonant	voiced final consonant
rope	*robe*
mop	*mob*
back	*bag*
heartbeat	*hard bead*
leaf	*leave*
price	*prize*
batch	*badge*

You may notice that voiceless final consonants shorten the preceding vowel, and voiced final consonants lengthen it. This does not apply in some languages, and carried into English such non-differentiation can cause mishearings, because in listening we often tend to be guided by the length of the vowel as much as by the consonant in end position, which is never as prominent as it would be in initial position (say *gag* or listen to it in an online dictionary and notice the difference between the two 'g's).

German in effect has no final voiced consonants, and consequently those L1 learners may unwittingly give the impression of abruptness when they use voiceless (tense) final consonants with shortened preceding vowels instead of voiced (lax) ones with lengthened preceding vowels. But recently I found myself correcting *We won first price* in a Spanish student's written work – proof perhaps that this difficulty is experienced by all learners whose L1's have constant vowel length, and again proof that phonemic correction benefits not only the spoken skill.

I have often been asked by a learner (no, not the same one) how to differentiate between *price* and *prize*. This difficulty is commonly noticed because of the high frequency of those words, but listen out for less frequent pairs that tend to go under the radar and correct as required. Business English students especially may not want to import *ropes* or have them brought up to their room by housekeeping but that's what they could end up with instead of the requested *robes*.

For correcting, write the mispronounced word with its partner, but condense the vowel before the voiceless consonant and stretch out the one before the voiced consonant. Then drill the words in phrases and sentences, adding a little role play if desirable. There's no need to use the phonemes, they're not much help here; wherever normal orthography carries the message don't be tempted to show off with them. The examples below include a little drawing. Remember to involve Ss as you draw or write: let them guess what you are drawing; let them finish the sentence you are writing or fill in a gap or two.

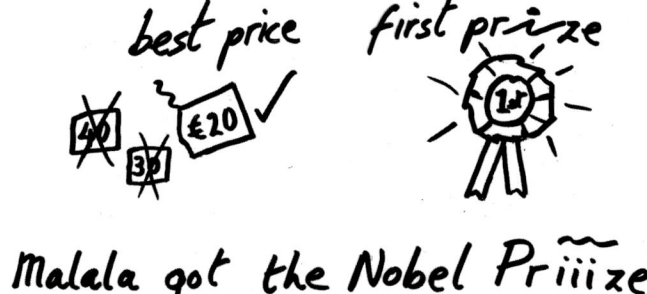

Figure 20: Condensed and expanded vowel letter, demonstrating the influence of the final voiceless and voiced consonant. Also, an example sentence with another way of 'stretching' the vowel. Example sentences are best when meaningful.

6.9 Role play script: voiceless/voiced final consonant

With practice, you and your students will be able to write good role-play scripts. This is not a practice book but we make an exception with role play because we believe that for enjoyable pronunciation practice there's nothing to beat it. Students should learn scripts off by heart and take turns performing to the class but only as much as classmates wish. Award prices, sorry, prizes.

TV Producer *(on the phone)*: Hello, is that the Supply Department?
Props Manager: Yes, how may I help you?
TVP: I need a mop for the next scene in a drama I'm doing.
PM: A mop?
TVP: Yes, a mop. Not too big, it's a group of strikers, a bit violent.
PM: Oh, are they cleaners?
TVP: What?
PM: Are they cleaners? You know, with the mop?
TVP: That doesn't matter.
PM: I think it *does* matter; I know I'm not a producer but…
TVP: For goodness sake, just organise the mop! Tomorrow, studio 7 at 2pm.
PM: Whatever you say. Goodbye. *(To herself)* He's very rude. I'll take that mop to him personally tomorrow and I'll tell him what to do with it!

Admittedly, the role play above doesn't have any sounding of *mob*, but this is not necessarily a negative; indeed, students will highlight the difference when explaining the joke to each other. Here's one with voiced and voiceless examples:

(Set the scene: backstage in a theatre or function room. Props: large receipt; handbag if the assistant is female.)
Prize giver: Have you got the prize?
Assistant: Yes, it's in my pocket (/handbag/purse).
P: Oh, I thought it would be bigger, but anyway, let's go. We're on next.
(They walk to a wing of the stage.)
P: Ok, here we are. We walk to the centre, ok, go *(they walk)*… and …
"Congratulations, Ms Jones, and here is your prize." *(Gestures to A.)*
(Audience (classmates) *applaud. Miss Jones beams at them, holds out her hands to A, gets nothing.)*
A: But boss…
P: Just take it out of your pocket (/handbag/purse); the cameras are rolling.
A: But boss…
P: *(Smiling awkwardly at the audience)* Take out the prize and give it to her.
A: Ok *(takes out a receipt)*. Here's the price: sixty euro. *(Ms Jones is aghast).*
P: The prize, the prize.
A: Yes, the price is very good, isn't it? But why didn't you want the trophy?

6.10 The schwa: /ə/

letter, doctor, cellar, about, o'clock, comfortable, desperate, camera, disposable, responsible, cactus.

One phoneme is essential on all courses: the schwa (the only phoneme with a name), otherwise known as 'the weak vowel', and all teachers are obliged to be fully aware of its functions in English. I shan't go into detail on this, but you'll know how difficult it is to spell a word like /'definət/. Is it *definite* or *definate*? And maybe you've been castigated for spelling *grammar* as *grammer*? The difficulty is caused by the fact that the final vowel in these words is the weak (or reduced) vowel, which can be represented by any vowel letter (though the letters *i* and *u* can perform as weak vowels in their own right). To pronounce the schwa just have your mouth slightly open and relaxed, raise the body of your tongue just a little and vibrate your vocal chords very briefly. There you have it, but it's best practised in or between words of course, because it never exists as a single utterance, like a letter of the alphabet can.

Learners without a weak vowel in their L1 will tend to give equal prominence to all vowels in English. To rectify this make sure when drilling that your 'conducting' hand is up just briefly for the schwa before coming down for the next stressed syllable. The rhythm of English is highly influenced by the schwa (there would be five 'down beats' in that preceding statement). Make sure you 'conduct' with that in mind. When including the schwa in a line of text on the board, make sure it is in a smaller size than the other letters. See figure 21.

Your coursebook will have ample practice for students. And the main activity in these tends to be a listening one, where Ss underline the syllables or letters where the schwa is heard. Another activity involving awareness but also production of the schwa uses a text in which all letters normally pronounced with it are substituted with an asterisk, for example:

> Thanks t* Jon*th*n Marks *nd Tim Bow*n f*r this ide* tak*n fr*m *Th* Book *f Pr*nunciati*n: Pr*pos*ls f*r * Practic*l Ped*gogy* (p84). Stud*nts rec*nstruct th* text by replacing the ast*risks with th* usu*l lett*rs *f the alph*bet. Then they read it *loud *nd check. They c*n also *dapt *noth*r text simil*rly. Y* c*d do it with * non-rhotic acc*nt, b*t mine h*s the 'r's'.

36 Essential Phonetics

7 Suprasegmentals

Suprasegmentals or *prosody* are terms used to describe the sounds 'above the segments', above the phonemes. These include mainly stress (within words), rhythm (= sentence stress. i.e. which words are stressed in a sentence, forming rhythm) and intonation.

7.1 Stress/emphasis, rhythm

Stress is a matter of volume/sonority, vowel length, pitch, and pulses of air from the lungs, more difficult to explain than simply demonstrate, so just demonstrate.

Spoken English is stress-timed: the beat falls on the stressed syllables only. Spanish, French, Chinese and more are syllable-timed: every syllable gets a beat. As you may know, content words, i.e. nouns, verbs, adjectives, adverbs and negatives, have a stressed syllable. The other words in their normal use don't, being pronounced with a weak vowel (the schwa /ə/ or the weak /ɪ/ or /u/); these are function words, i.e. (most) prepositions, the articles, conjunctions, linking verb *be*, auxiliary verbs (not negated). Also, pronouns (except *I* and *they*).

Below is how a sentence can be presented on the board, showing the weak syllables (with a schwa) written small and the stressed syllables written large. There's usually no need to transcribe (write in phonemes) more than the weak vowels, especially when rhythm is the objective. There are actually three degrees of stress in English, which we shall meet in 7.5. And perhaps I should add here that many of the board writing examples in this book are as they might be seen on a busy teacher's board.

*You can LEAD ə HORSE to WATər
but yə CAN'T MAKE it DRINK.*

Figure 21: Weak vowel and stress marking. The indefinite pronoun *you* is normally pronounced with the weak vowel /ju/ or /jə/, especially the latter when repeated, as shown above, or in casual register. Also included is the linking of *make it drink*, and the (rising-) falling intonation line with the stress mark over *drink*.

7.2 Contrastive stress

If they provide 'new' information (see 8.3) in the sentence, e.g. *From east to west...*, or contrast with a corresponding word, e.g. *sent from the office, not to the office*, function words will be pronounced with their full prominence. Pronouns are treated similarly, but *I* can be heard as /a/ especially in GA, e.g.

   a *just don't know what's wrong but* **a** *guess it'll be okay.*

7.3 Pronouns, and the conjunction *that*

The lines below consist of a sentence with its phonemic transcription in a GB, then a GA accent. Note the alveolar tap [t̬], as explained in 1.3. The italic schwa /*ə*/ in *them* indicates it may be omitted.

   What he didn't know was that I saw them at the station.
GB: wɒt i dɪdn   nəʊ   wəz ðət aɪ sɔː   ðəm ət ðə ˈsteɪʃən
GA: wɑt̬ i dɪdn   noʊ   wəz ðət̬ aɪ sɑː   ðəm ət ðə ˈsteɪʃən

Below is the same sentence as written on the board for pronunciation practice, perhaps following from hearing pronouns pronounced too prominently, and hearing *that* stressed as a demonstrative pronoun or adjective rather than unstressed as the conjunction it is here.

*Whát (h)e didn͜know wəs
ðət Í sáw ðəm͜ət͜ðə státiən.*

Figure 22: Stress marking, weak vowels and linking of some words.

Note that in the above the spelling of 'he' is retained (with the 'h' in parentheses) as neither the phoneme /i/ or the letter 'e' in isolation would be instantly decodable. The *What* would have variable stress depending on the context. The *I* is stressed as it is 'new' (not occurring in the previous utterance or predictable in this one). The phoneme /ð/ is used for the 'th' in *the* as it reduces the size of the word, with the intention of reducing its vocal prominence. The weak vowel in *station* wouldn't normally need inclusion as students tend to pronounce this word correctly, it being so common.

7.4 Marking the stressed syllables

Some TEFL teacher trainers may direct that each stressed syllable be marked on the board with a box or circle above it. This can be time consuming and I would prefer the simplicity of a thick accent mark, and/or writing the stressed syllables larger than the others while writing (see figure 21). However, for activities such as identifying (and then imitating) the stress pattern of a word or phrase, circles of two or more sizes perform well. And some students seem to derive much fun from hearing the teacher go 'DAH-DAH-di-DAH-di' and suchlike (= Thánk Gód it's Frídáy).

If you like, you can put a list of popular movies (or whatever Ss may be familiar with) on the board; give each student a card with the name of a movie, stress-marked, on it. Each student takes a turn doing the DAH-di-DAH and the others guess the movie. Then you could reveal the stress marks and title for all to see, and drill as required.

I prefer reality to nonsense words for practice, reviewing known phrases or doing quiz-like activities, e.g. can you write in the names of the national airlines below? One includes the word *airlines*, one is based in the Middle East, three are European, and two don't use the country's name. The one in row number 4 could be spoken with primary stress on the first syllable, the third stress becoming secondary. Normally two stress levels are enough for practice, but I've included three here by way of interest, and probable argument: primary, secondary, and weak, as indicated by the size of the circles. The answers are at the end of this chapter.

0	o O o O	Korean Air
1	O o o	
2	O O	
3	O o o	
4	o o O O o	
5	o o O o	
6	O o	

Figure 23: Stress patterns of names of airlines. Answers at the end of the chapter.

7.5 Three degrees of stress

There are three stress levels in English, marked in dictionaries so:

primary, marked with a preceding (up-placed) apostrophe;
secondary, marked with a preceding down-placed apostrophe;
weak, represented by the schwa /ə/.

The /ɪ/ and /u/ may also be pronounced weak in certain environments. Observe:

Dictionary entry: in•tui•tive	in•tu•ition
Stress marking: /ɪn'tjuːɪtɪv/	/ˌɪntju'ɪʃn/
Alternative: /ɪn'tjuːətɪv/	/ˌɪntju'ɪʃən/

In *intuitive* the first syllable is weak, the second syllable /'tjuːɪ/ has primary stress ('confirmed' by the full-length /uː/), and the final syllable /tɪv/ is also weak.

In *intuition* the first syllable /ˌɪn/ has secondary stress, the second syllable /tju/ is weak, and the third syllable /'ɪʃn/ has primary stress.

Some dictionaries may show alternative pronunciations. The smaller schwa size indicates it may be omitted.

In dictionary entries the dots (•) show where the word may be broken; this gives an indication of syllable juncture, but there is rarely full agreement on such, and rarely a need for close analysis in ELT.

GA does not normally have a /j/ glide after a /t/, hence /ɪn'tuɪtɪv/. This parallels the *news* /nuːz/ 'nooz' versus /njuːz/ 'nee-ooz' difference. It is also related to the /suː/ vs /sjuː/ in *supermarket*, etc, but the latter has declined in use. In other varieties or in fast speech /tju/ may be pronounced as /t͡ʃ/, noticeable when *Tuesday* is pronounced as 'chewsday', etc.

Again, the above stress marking convention is that of dictionaries; most teachers seem to prefer an acute accent over the relevant syllable in text on the board. And normally it's only necessary to mark the primary stresses – secondary stress placement seems to be learnt in tandem without much conscious effort. That said, it is important to have a knowledge of both types for when the need arises (there is an instance of when a grave accent is useful in 7.8 below).

7.6 Stress in words

There are some rules about where the stress falls in words, but apart from noun-verb distinction, e.g. *cónduct* vs *condúct*, *pérmit* vs *permít*, *óbject* vs *objéct*, I've rarely had to mention them because students seem to prefer learning word pronunciation in the normal run of lessons. But of course exercises with patterns like *vérsatile ~ versatílity*, *pérsonal ~ personálity* (primary stress movement to the pre-suffix syllable) can be found in suitable vocabulary practice media and fulfil a certain need. During reading aloud, after you've corrected a student's pronunciation of an important word (showing the correct form on the board) ask them to mark the stressed syllable in their book/handout. Yes, reading aloud, properly done, is an excellent way to check pronunciation (Penston 2011).

7.7 Phrasal verbs

The idiomaticity of phrasal verbs presents a challenge in their learning, but there is also an important aspect about their pronunciation: the majority of phrasal verbs have secondary stress on the verb and primary stress on the particle. I usually mark the stress solely on the particle, thus: *Move ón!* This is very different from the *on* in *Móve on the dance floor* (preposition phrase underlined), but of course the particle looks exactly the same as that common preposition, and the learner is forgiven for thinking that verbs are more important than the little words that may follow them.

7.8 Compounds

Compounds may need some care. After teaching that *státion* has primary stress on the first syllable you might be surprised to find that this is not so in *políce státion* (noun + noun type), where it has secondary stress. There is also a compound that has two primary stresses, e.g. *páper tíger* (material + noun type).

Compounds are not to be confused with descriptive adjective + noun pairings, like *a big státion*. However, with these it is still necessary to ensure that the adjective gets its proper stress, as some Ss leave it quite weak, due perhaps to L1 interference.

Answers to quiz on page 39:
1 Lufthansa, 2 Air France, 3 Emirates, 4 Singapore Airlines, 5 British Airways. 6 Qantas.

8 Intonation

8.1 Tone movements and meanings

The pitch/tone of our voice generally falls at the end of a statement and wh- question. It generally rises at the end of a yes/no question. It also rises at the end of a statement to turn it into a question or register surprise, at the end of a (repeated) wh- question to check the received information, and at the end of a tag question when it is really a question and not a conversational remark. Other tone movements are rise-fall, fall-rise and level pitch, and of course these can all vary in degree. Much of these movements and their meanings would seem to be universal, but learners coming from tonal languages (e.g. Chinese, where a word can have one of a possible four phonemic tones) may take a little time getting used to the L2 system; German L1 students may use a fall-rise at the end of an answer instead of the (rise-) fall, unwittingly sounding dismissive; learners whose L1's syntax has the 'topic' words in very different places from those in English will also need time to get 'in tune' with the new patterns.

8.2 The tonic syllable

Utterances are broken into ***tone groups***. A tone group may consist of one word, but is usually a phrase. In a tone group one syllable will have a noticeable change in pitch/tone; this is called the ***tonic syllable***. The tonic syllable is usually towards the end of the tone group. The part before the tonic may also contain stressed syllables but they won't be tonic.

> Whén are you cóming HOME?
> I'm cóming hóme toMORrow.

In both of the above sentences there is a (rise-) fall on the tonic syllable (in capital letters). In the second, the fall continues through -*row*.

Of course, although there is general agreement on tone pattern there are degrees of personal and regional variance; for me, a final falling tone is really a high rise-fall, and many GA and AuE speakers use high rises throughout narratives as a 'are you with me' check. The rise, especially in the case of adolescents, can also apply to the final tonic in statements, but its purpose there is not quite discernible (Liberman

2006). For all varieties there are small movements which can be important; for example, in the sentences above there could be a slight rise at the end to indicate friendliness. This slight rise can also be used at the end of a wh-question or request to show deference, e.g.

> Whén are the SALary incréases dúe?

Tone movements are shown in most academic books with small arrows before the tone group, but on the board it's better to simply draw a line above the sentence. Drill as you trace the intonation line. When you face your Ss to 'conduct' the drill be careful to 'draw' the line in the air from right to left, not the other direction.

There would seem to be two tonic syllables in the proverb *An apple a day keeps the doctor away*, shown on the intonation line now. There's hardly any tone change on the non-tonic stressed syllables (i.e. in *ápple, kéeps, dóctor*), but they are marked with a small rise to distinguish them from the weak sounds.

An apple a day keeps the doctor away.

Figure 24. Sentence with two tone groups. The tone direction on *day* could be falling rather than rising; if you use a falling tone then draw the line dipping into the text. The rises (or falls) over the tonics dispense with the need to put these in caps.

8.3 Given and new information

(From now on falling and rising tones should be understood as commonly beginning with a rise and fall respectively). We have seen above that in the answer I'm cóming hóme toMORrow the matter of the *coming home* is 'given/known' information. This is spoken with a rising tone. The *tomorrow* is 'new', spoken with a falling tone. Related to this is how a continuous tense (background information) will often have a rising tone, while the main event has a falling tone. How *An apple a day* above would undergo this attribution is unclear; would the rising tone signal background or 'known' information, or would it be saying 'hold on, there's more'? And when someone uses a falling tone on *day* are they presenting this as 'new' information? Possibly.

8.4 Try storytelling

The signalling of information structure by intonation, inasmuch as it occurs, appears to be in need of an agreed, transparent model (Levis 2014). Indeed intonation is a difficult subject to teach definitively, but this is not to say that intonation is not being learned in most lessons, for indeed it is, anytime there is speech. Storytelling is perhaps the best way to practise all tones; make sure you exploit it, for all ages.

8.5 'Ham up' role play for intonation practice

Coursebook audios, video extracts (with subtitles available, preferably) and additional listening materials are useful for raising awareness of intonation, but do also use role play for practice, because the 'hamming up' which is essential in most sketches is very valuable and good fun. The following oldie, adapted for ELT some time ago in *Fun Class Activities 2* (Watcyn-Jones) always gets a laugh, but you must rehearse the actors in their exaggerated intonation before any performance.

I've had three husbands. They all died.
Three husbands! How unfortunate.
My first husband, Fred, he died of poisoned mushrooms.
Oh my goodness! How terrible.
And my second husband, Siegfried, he went the same way.
Poisoned mushrooms?! Well, I never. You can't be too careful, can you?
My third husband died of a broken skull.
Oh dear! How did that happen?
He wouldn't eat his mushrooms.

I am also reminded of a scene in *Fawlty Towers**, which left my students crooning "Oh, I know" with hilarious rise-fall-rise-fall for weeks:

He terrified me, Mrs Fawlty.
Oh, I know.
His hand. The dark. it was so horrible.
Oh, I know.
Anything could have happened.
He *was* dead, dear.
A man's a man, Mrs Fawlty!
Oh, I know.

*Cleese & Booth, 2000, p263. With apologies for the simplification.

9 Accent

9.1 Teachers have different accents

The subject of accent in pronunciation teaching is a vexed one, there being so many accents used by English teachers, yet only one, usually the 'prestige' or standard, used in their coursebook's pronunciation practice and testing sections. The ability to switch accents on the coursebook audio may soon become possible, but until then teachers have to decide how to approach phonemic practice sections which use an accent different from their own.

Some teachers skip the pronunciation sections in their coursebooks. This may be out of fear of not knowing how to explain differences in accent, a problem which we would hope this booklet can cure, or simply because they believe that phonemic awareness exercises have low priority in communicative language teaching.

If your accent is not GB try doing the following 'odd one out' phonemic practice test, similar to those in a small number of (British) coursebooks. The answers are at the bottom of the page.

	1	2	3	4	Phoneme
A	wrote	wore	caught	saw	___
B	man	mark	star	cast	___
C	work	permanent	short	early	___
D	luck	comfort	plug	put	___

Figure 25. 'Odd one out' phonemic discrimination practice test.

9.2 Native speaker accent

Most of the communication in English is done between non-native speakers; therefore, there is no need for a learner to achieve a native speaker accent. Conversely, it would seem beneficial for native speakers to become more aware of a 'Lingua Franca' accent for global communication (Walker, 2010). Clarity of speech, evidenced by causing few if any breakdowns in communication, is the objective in ELT pronunciation teaching.

Answers to 'odd one out': A1, B1, C3 and D4. The phonemes are, in descending order, /ɔː/, /ɑː/, /ɜː/ and /ʌ/.

10 Using phonemes in class

10.1 To dispel ambiguity

I don't recommend the gratuitous teaching of phonemes. However, English spelling being what it is phonemes can offer an unambiguous representation of sound when required. This was instanced with diphthongs above (6.6-7). We would also posit that certain phonemes (not all – the grapheme 'sh' for example is preferable over the symbol /ʃ/) can act as combined visual mnemonics and speech motor guides when shown in vowel charts and/or in tandem with relevant vocal tract diagrams (which you can draw). Salient examples of words to benefit from phonemic transcription would be *cute* /kjuːt/, *cut* /kʌt/, *cushion* /kʊshn/; *woman* /wʊmən/, *women* /wɪmɪn/ (my use of 'sh' rather than /ʃ/ in /kʊshn/ here, also non-use of stress marks, is deliberate). A further example follows.

of and *off*

Some students ask about the difference in pronunciation between *of* and *off*. Obviously the written form offers little help, indeed as in many cases it can be the cause of the difficulty. Students may be focusing on the double consonant and missing the real differences, which include the schwa /ə/ and /v/ for *of*, and the vowel length in *off*. In the example boardwork below, the /ð/ for the voiced 'th' sound in *the* is not required to be taught, but it does make the word look shorter, thereby signalling weaker stress. For lower levels the wording would be easier, e.g. *the start of the revolution; they started off in Argentina / they fell off the bike.*

Attenborough answered the call of the wild.
He ánswered ðə cáll əv ðə wíld.

The ref. had to call off the match.
He had to cáll ɔːf ðə mátch.

Figure 26. Boardwork showing the difference in pronunciation between *of* and *off*. Syllables with primary stress are in larger size and/or given an accent mark. Context is paramount in communicative language teaching, so target words are put into meaningful sentences for practice.

THE INTERNATIONAL PHONETIC ALPHABET (revised to 2005)

CONSONANTS (PULMONIC)

© 2005 IPA

	Bilabial	Labiodental	Dental	Alveolar	Postalveolar	Retroflex	Palatal	Velar	Uvular	Pharyngeal	Glottal
Plosive	p b			t d		ʈ ɖ	c ɟ	k ɡ	q ɢ		ʔ
Nasal	m	ɱ		n		ɳ	ɲ	ŋ	ɴ		
Trill	B			r					R		
Tap or Flap		ⱱ		ɾ		ɽ					
Fricative	ɸ β	f v	θ ð	s z	ʃ ʒ	ʂ ʐ	ç ʝ	x ɣ	χ ʁ	ħ ʕ	h ɦ
Lateral fricative				ɬ ɮ							
Approximant		ʋ		ɹ		ɻ	j	ɰ			
Lateral approximant				l		ɭ	ʎ	ʟ			

Where symbols appear in pairs, the one to the right represents a voiced consonant. Shaded areas denote articulations judged impossible.

CONSONANTS (NON-PULMONIC)

Clicks	Voiced implosives	Ejectives
ʘ Bilabial	ɓ Bilabial	ʼ Examples:
ǀ Dental	ɗ Dental/alveolar	pʼ Bilabial
ǃ (Post)alveolar	ʄ Palatal	tʼ Dental/alveolar
ǂ Palatoalveolar	ɠ Velar	kʼ Velar
ǁ Alveolar lateral	ʛ Uvular	sʼ Alveolar fricative

OTHER SYMBOLS

- ʍ Voiceless labial-velar fricative
- w Voiced labial-velar approximant
- ɥ Voiced labial-palatal approximant
- ʜ Voiceless epiglottal fricative
- ʢ Voiced epiglottal fricative
- ʡ Epiglottal plosive
- ɕ ʑ Alveolo-palatal fricatives
- ɺ Voiced alveolar lateral flap
- ɧ Simultaneous ʃ and x

Affricates and double articulations can be represented by two symbols joined by a tie bar if necessary.

k͡p t͡s

VOWELS

```
            Front        Central        Back
Close       i • y        ɨ • ʉ          ɯ • u
                    I Y          ʊ
Close-mid   e • ø        ɘ • ɵ          ɤ • o
                         ə
Open-mid    ɛ • œ        ɜ • ɞ          ʌ • ɔ
                         æ    ɐ
Open        a • ɶ                       ɑ • ɒ
```

Where symbols appear in pairs, the one to the right represents a rounded vowel.

SUPRASEGMENTALS

- ˈ Primary stress
- ˌ Secondary stress ˌfoʊnəˈtɪʃən
- ː Long   eː
- ˑ Half-long eˑ
- ˘ Extra-short ĕ
- | Minor (foot) group
- ‖ Major (intonation) group
- . Syllable break ɹi.ækt
- ‿ Linking (absence of a break)

TONES AND WORD ACCENTS

LEVEL		CONTOUR	
ə̋ or ˥	Extra high	ě or ˬ	Rising
é ˦	High	ê ˯	Falling
ē ˧	Mid	e̋ ˫	High rising
è ˨	Low	ȅ ˪	Low rising
ə̏ ˩	Extra low	e᷈ ˮ	Rising-falling
↓	Downstep	↗	Global rise
↑	Upstep	↘	Global fall

DIACRITICS

Diacritics may be placed above a symbol with a descender, e.g. ŋ̊

̥ Voiceless	n̥ d̥	̤ Breathy voiced	b̤ a̤	̪ Dental	t̪ d̪
̬ Voiced	s̬ t̬	̰ Creaky voiced	b̰ a̰	̺ Apical	t̺ d̺
ʰ Aspirated	tʰ dʰ	̼ Linguolabial	t̼ d̼	̻ Laminal	t̻ d̻
̹ More rounded	ɔ̹	ʷ Labialized	tʷ dʷ	̃ Nasalized	ẽ
̜ Less rounded	ɔ̜	ʲ Palatalized	tʲ dʲ	ⁿ Nasal release	dⁿ
̟ Advanced	u̟	ˠ Velarized	tˠ dˠ	ˡ Lateral release	dˡ
̠ Retracted	e̠	ˤ Pharyngealized	tˤ dˤ	̚ No audible release	d̚
̈ Centralized	ë	̴ Velarized or pharyngealized	ɫ		
̽ Mid-centralized	ë	̝ Raised	e̝ (ɹ̝ = voiced alveolar fricative)		
̩ Syllabic	n̩	̞ Lowered	e̞ (β̞ = voiced bilabial approximant)		
̯ Non-syllabic	e̯	̘ Advanced Tongue Root	e̘		
˞ Rhoticity	ə˞ a˞	̙ Retracted Tongue Root	e̙		

IPA Chart, http://www.langsci.ucl.ac.uk/ipa/ipachart.html, available under a Creative Commons Attribution-Sharealike 3.0 Unported License. Copyright © 2005 International Phonetic Association.

BIBLIOGRAPHY

*Titles marked with an asterisk consist largely of learner pronunciation activities.

*Baker, A. (2006) *Ship or Sheep?* Cambridge University Press.
Bent, T. & Bradlow, A. R. (2003) 'The interlanguage speech intelligibility benefit'. *Acoustical Society of America* Vol 114/3 1600-1610.
Celce-Murcia, M. et al (2010) *Teaching Pronunciation; A Course Book and Reference Guide*. Cambridge University Press (New York).
Cleese, J. & Booth, C. (2000) *The Complete Fawlty Towers*. Methuen.
Cruttenden, A. (2014) *Gimson's Pronunciation of English*. Routledge.
Duanmu, S. (2007) *The Phonology of Standard Chinese*. Oxford University Press.
Fry, D. B. (1947) 'The frequency of occurrence of speech sounds in southern English'. *Archives Néerlandaises de Phonétique Expérimentale* 20, 103-106.
*Hancock, M. (2012) *English Pronunciation in Use – Intermediate* (2nd ed.) Cambridge University Press.
Heaney, S. (1980) *Selected Poems 1965-1975*. 'Viking Dublin: Trial Pieces', p109. Faber & Faber.
Jenkins, J. (2000) *The Phonology of English as a Lingua Franca*. Oxford University Press.
*Kenworthy, J. (1987) *Teaching English Pronunciation*. Longman.
Ladefoged, P. (2000) *A Course in Phonetics*. Heinle & Heinle.
Liberman, M. (2006) 'Uptalk is not HRT'.
  http://itre.cis.upenn.edu/~myl/languagelog/archives/002967.html
Macpherson, I. R. (1980) *Spanish Phonology: Descriptive and Historical*. Manchester University Press.
*Marks, J. & Bowen, T. (2012) *The Book of Pronunciation: Proposals for a Practical Pedagogy*. Delta Publishing.
Parker, R. & Graham, T. (2002) *An Introduction to the Phonology of English for Teachers of ESOL*. ELB Publishing.
Penston, T. (2011) 'Learner-centredness and reading aloud'. *Modern English Teacher* Vol 20/3 46-48.
Roach, S. (2009) *English Phonetics and Phonology*. Cambridge University Press.
Swan, M. & Smith, B. (eds) (2001) *Learner English*. Cambridge University Press.
Underhill, A. (2005) *Sound Foundations*. Macmillan.
Vance, T. J. (2008) *The Sounds of Japanese*. Cambridge University Press.
*Vaughan-Rees, M. *Rhymes and Rhythm*. Garnet 2010.
Walter, C. (2008) 'Phonology in second language reading: not an optional extra'. *TESOL Quarterly* Vol 42/3 455-474.
Walker, R. (2010) *Teaching the Pronunciation of English as a Lingua Franca*. Oxford University Press.
Watcyn-Jones, P. (2004) *Fun Class Activities 2*. Pearson.
Wells, J.C. (1982) *Accents of English 2 : The British Isles*. Cambridge University Press.